Ioannis Tzivanakis

AF208768

# ADHD
# decoded

ITV

Publisher: Ioannis Tzivanakis Verlag, Hamburg 2018.

Printed in Germany.

ISBN 978-3-940493-14-9

**www.adhddecoded.com**

Bibliographic information published by the Deutsche
Nationalbibliothek (German National Library): The Deutsche
Nationalbibliothek lists this publication in the Deutsche
Nationalbibliografie (German National Bibliography).

# Contents

-------------------------------------------------------------------------

For Inghard

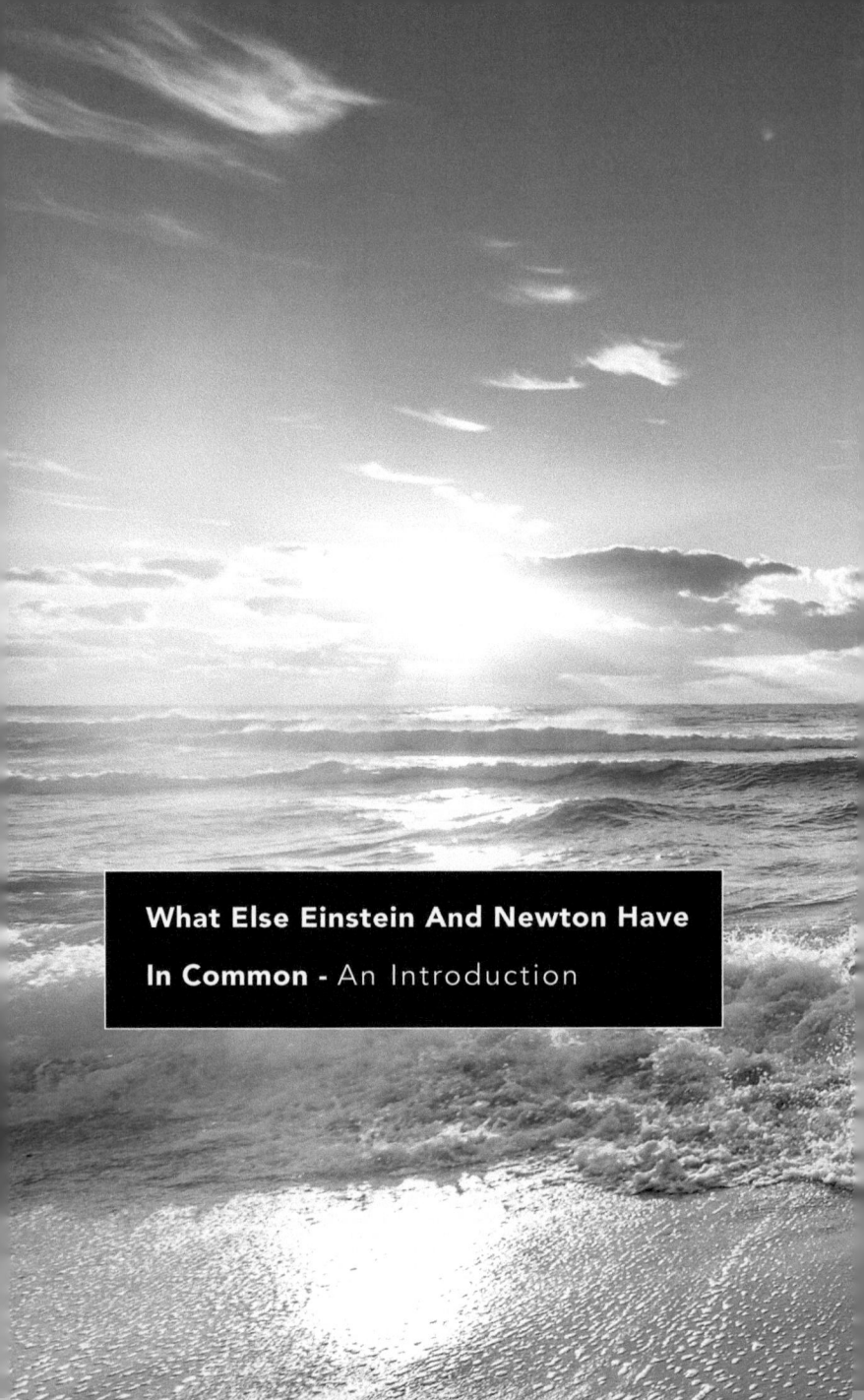

**What Else Einstein And Newton Have In Common -** An Introduction

"I don't know how the others see me, but I myself feel like a little boy who plays on the beach and is happy when he finds a particularly smooth pebble or a particularly beautiful shell here and there, while the great ocean of truth is completely undiscovered in front of him."

Isaac Newton

## What Else Einstein And Newton Have In Common - An Introduction

"We just keep getting better at what we like and what we just do more often. I think this is one of the secrets that helped Einstein to find out everything," I said to one of my clients (11 years old) about 12 years ago when we talked about having fun with learning. His reaction was prompt.

"Ahh, Einstein," he replied. Now I became curious.

"How? What do you mean by that? You know him well? Not personally, I mean."

"Yes, personally," he said. "Well, no, I don't know him personally. But!... I know someone who somehow knew him personally..."

I smiled at him and felt how he visibly enjoyed waiting for me to ask.

"Ohhh!" was my reaction, "do you want to tell me?"

He nodded a 'yes', waited for a moment and then he told me...

"Well, not even that. My father told me. My great-grandfather, my father's grandfather, was sitting with Einstein in the same school class in Munich."

"Really?"

"Yes!"

I have to admit, I clearly felt goose bumps inside me. And as if I was supposed to use this moment immediately, I felt, I asked directly.

"Wow!...," I said and asked: "And had he said anything about him? Your great-grandfather, I mean, about Einstein?"

The father of my client was also sitting at the table and was already nodding.

"Well, just tell!" he told his son.

"Well, he said that Einstein slept or dreamt almost all the time, he had no interest in what was happening in the classroom."

"Well, so it is, isn't it? I've heard that before."

"Yes, but he also said, as soon as it was about physics or math, Einstein was not only interested, but stronger than the teachers."

"Wow...," I could only say.

Apart from how this conversation with my client went on, all this was reason enough for me to finally get myself an Einstein biography. I wanted to know every-thing a little more exactly...

I also acquired Isaac Newtons biography. Not only were they both gigantic in their contribution to the science of physics, but they were driven deeply within by the magical power of the miracle inherent in the entire manifestation, which is appearing, touching and challenging the human mind and its need to understand. And they have strongly devoted themselves to this drive...

About Newton: "He carved sundials into stones and recorded the shadows cast by their pointers on a map. This meant to see time as being related to space, duration as length, the length of an arc. He measured small distances with twine and translated the minutes of an hour into inches."

About Einstein: "While his contemporaries chase adventures outside, inside he seeks his "flow experience" in his head...

...His extremely vital relatives see a small Buddha sitting on the sofa, absent, meditating on questions of mathematics as if in a trance."

It would be fatal, or at least inappropriate, if we thought of sticking the *ADHD* label on such minds just because they were often mentally *somewhere else* than most of their "peers" were most often.

Newton and Einstein were highly aware of where they were mentally and what they were doing or what they were opening up to.

And by no means does this mean that they had lost contact with concrete and practical reality.

*Conscious will* has guided them decisively; not *al-*

*ways* perhaps and not totally, but *very strongly*.

The force at work here is one of several forces that entirely *determine* our will and the will that constitutes us.

This book is about *understanding* these forces and how their different proportions can lead to an *imbalance* in our state of mind and the ability to control our lives, which can then also be called ADHD, whether erroneously or with a certain right.

Why? So that the imbalance can be *eliminated*. Because ADHD can be deciphered and its undesirable facets can be resolved.

And how do I get this knowledge? Through (past) *personal* ADHD experience, through working with many affected people and not least because of my strong interest in the *phenomenon* of attention, for thirty years now.

Why is the phenomenon of attention so *special*?

What *is* attention?

What is ADHD *not*?

What is ADHD *really*?

To what extent is ADHD related to *life as a whole*?

How can ADHD be *eliminated* or *dissolved* with regard to its problematic facets?

I wanted to keep this book short, but leave nothing

out that is necessary to understand ADHD and (1) to "handle" it accordingly as well as (2) to discover and use the transformative power that lies in the understanding of ADHD.

The book is intended to help ensure that no short-term strategies are pursued at the surface of symptoms, but that the *fundamental* changes are uncovered, which are *feelingly* and therefore *truly necessary*.

"To control attention means to control the experience and thus the quality of life."

Mihaly Csikszentmihalyi

# PART I - The Phenomenon Of *Attention*

# 1. Why Is Attention Important?

What does really happen when you read these lines? Are you aware of it? Or are you just attentive to it? Or both? And if both, in what order? Or is both the same?

These questions are or become important if one is really interested in the phenomenon of attention. So what are the reasons that underline the importance of this phenomenon?

The explosively multi-layered and multi-shaped development and changeability of the 21st century, both in the technological, scientific and social fields and in the more diverse forms of experience, can cause both an overload of information processing and a cloudiness of the ability to make decisions. Not that in earlier times everything was simpler and easier, but an intensification, enrichment and dynamization of what becomes and is available and its speed cannot be denied by our time.

The understanding of attention as a central function of our organismic existence, especially in its outstanding instrumentality for a conscious and balanced life, is more urgent than ever. Why? There are two main reasons.

If I am not aware of something, *I do not experience it*. And the second reason...

While I am attentive to something, *anything else* that I might be attentive to *at the same time is excluded*; it does *not exist* within my experience!...

Since our time is not infinite, it becomes clear at a stroke why both time and attention are our most important resources.

As far as time is concerned, it is already given how long a day-and-night cycle of time is and how long, under today's technological state of affairs, a whole life. In this sense, we cannot change so much about the dimension of time - apart from what science and technology (in the future) could still do...

As far as attention is concerned, however, there is much we can very well and very much (now) change.

It is not so easy to define 'attention', because this mechanism is so at the root of our perception that we must be very inclined to equate it with what is probably the most basic phenomenon that characterizes us as living beings or existing beings, unlike others: consciousness.

Indeed, it happens in research and among all those interested that there are different views on whether the phenomenon of attention precedes the phenomenon of consciousness or vice versa... Certainly, this is not done out of whims, but for good reasons.

Personally, I have little doubt as to the sequence in which these two phenomena must "follow" one another. Where my certainty comes from, I will show in the following explanations; thus my view would be open for a discussion.

Attention is a tool that we must use to observe something that is itself a *prerequisite* of this observation! At first it sounds like a paradoxical self-reference, a possibly logical loop-back in which we do not know what its beginning and end is.

That is why the question that immediately comes to mind here is this: Is it possible for me to observe myself by *exploring* my attention through focusing my *attention* on my *attention*?

Would such an attempt be as entangled as it sounds here? Not at all. My finding is even that both the <u>inseparability of our attention from our experience</u> must be recognized, as well as the <u>indispensable necessity of</u>

our <u>attention</u>, its <u>incessancy</u> and not least its <u>nature</u>, so that it can be illuminated holistically as it deserves.

## 2. Indispensable For Conscious Experience

In order to know that something has happened or that something is there, I must have *noticed* it. How else could I tell someone that it was raining, for example? I've seen and heard the rain or heard the rain dripping on my umbrella or felt the feet that got wet and cold from the rain. This fact seems self-evident, if not superfluous to mention.

Because it is impossible to *know* something that I did not *notice* and that I was not *aware* of.

Generally speaking, we could say that the real content of the term 'attention', i.e. the living event in which we experience attention by activating it as a basic function of our perception, is generally difficult to grasp because we are dealing here with a very basic, if not extremely basic, activity that is difficult to trace back to anything else.

Attention is fundamental in the sense that it is indispensable for conscious experience in the first place. One could almost *equate* 'attention' with the words 'conscious experience' or 'conscious perception'.

In other words: I only perceive something consciously or experience it consciously when my attention is directed to it, pointed at it. Or is it not?

If, for example, I look out of the window in a thoughtful, or dreamy moment, my physical eyes are on the tree in the garden while I think of my last holiday, I don't perceive a tree. The content of my conscious experience is my last holiday. And as soon as the motivational force for the holiday idea diminishes or exhausts itself, I only then - if another thought does not automatically creep in - could perceive the tree and its gentle movements in the light wind.

For *such reasons* I equate attention with *conscious* experience. And that is why it is so decisively fundamental for our experience, for the content of our existence and thus indirectly also for our way of life.

## 3. Unceasingly Active

Attention is also fundamental to our experience in that it is *incessantly* present, i.e. active.

It is always or continuously directed towards something. It can change the content of its orientation constantly or very often in the course of a day, an hour, or even within a minute or second, but it *always* has a content, an object. In other words, we are *constantly* aware of something. Even while we are sleeping and dreaming.

Whether awake or in a dream, whether we are alone or with others, whether we talk, or listen to others, whether we are physically or mentally active, whether we do something at all or even do nothing(!); we are constantly attentive to something. And this does not mean that we are only attentive to thoughts and images in our imagination, but also to sensations and to completely different physical states; or to the most diverse emotions; even to sometimes very subtle, very fine, inconceivable and unspeakable experiences...

So we might be able - there's nothing really proven; at least I can't prove it here - to consider as the only exception our state in deep sleep - or a "similar" state like the coma - during which we are not attentive to something, provided we don't dream while lying in a coma, or it's not a coma in which some level of awake consciousness is activated after all.

Except in the cases mentioned, there are only a few exceptional moments in the waking state in which we are not aware of anything. Such moments are possible during a change of state.

If, for example, after a rather long mental exertion, we come into the saving pleasure of a break and feel the whole mental effort suddenly collapse... In such a moment of relaxation the excitement of our attention can diminish so much that we – indirectly and retro-spectively observed – experience thoughtlessness for at least short moments; our attention is not focused on anything and therefore it is ...as good as "not there at all" or moves only extremely softly and unnoticed.

Or when we wake up from a deep sleep and we need a moment to be completely mentally active. In such a moment we are still half asleep with all our phys-ical energy. During this state, the necessary activation tension for the full functioning of our attention activity is not yet present.

This circumstance offers us another opportunity to feel what it is like when our attention is absent or lies fallow. We rest and are energetically certain to be present; we just don't notice anything; we don't even notice ourselves!

Also extreme feelings like fear or awestruck amazement or other intensive (also positive) experiences and sensations in general, which because of their intensity temporarily suspend our working mind, are able to switch off our attention.

The incessant stream of our attention is synonymous with the *entirety of our lifetime*. How we can affect this stream, how we can influence both its direction and the way it flows - these are *vitally significant* life questions.

"Every one knows what attention is. It is the taking possession by the mind, in clear and vivid form, of one out of what seem several simultaneously possible objects or trains of thought. Focalization, concentration, of consciousness are of its essence. It implies withdrawal from some things in order to deal effectively with others, and is a condition which has a real opposite in the confused, dazed, scatterbrained state which in French is called *distraction*, and *Zerstreutheit* in German."

William James

## 4. What Is Attention?

If we are attentive to something, according to William James (in the quote on the previous page) *our mind takes possession of that something*. The American Webster dictionary does not sound unsimilar when it says that *attention is the act or state in which we apply our mind to something*, one could also say here: use our mind for something.

What makes it more interesting is the explanation of 'mind' that Webster gives: *the element (or complex of elements) within us that feels, perceives, thinks, wants, and concludes*. And last but not least, Webster further states that 'mind' means *the conscious events and abilities in an organism*.

Whatever is meant by the term 'mind', depending on whether I am perceiving something with my senses or feeling it internally or even differently, I would rather first use the term 'subject of perception' to cover all possible channels and modes of perception. By 'subject' I mean that which is within me or from me, which is directed at an object. This is the case, for example, when our senses are active, so that the subject of perception uses one or the respective sense as a vehicle with which it directs itself towards an object. And 'mind' would also be included here insofar as senses are not only physically real, but also active in the mind (I hear a melody in my imagination, for example, even if physically there are no real sound waves that cause it).

Let's just try to identify the defining characteristics of 'attention'.

We first need the subject of perception, i.e. someone who "has" something like that, usually a sufficiently equipped living organism, then an object, something, and finally the event of the perceptual subject's alignment with that object.

The last sentence can now also serve as our basis for definition:

'Attention' thus means: the directedness of the subject of perception (of a correspondingly equipped living being) towards an object.

Again from the I-perspective:

'I am attentive' means: my or I as the subject of perception is or am directed towards an object. Or: As a subject of perception, I am directed towards something specific.

Let us now take a closer look at this definition by examining the three defining components: a) the perceptual subject, b) its directedness or directedness towards something, and c) the object, i.e. the object towards which the perceptual subject is directed.

a) In reality, there is no identifiable perceptual subject! This means that it is not a fixed quantity, but an energetic-functional entity, i.e. an energy condensation that arises under certain circumstances and has a certain function, fulfills a certain purpose and in different duration cycles.

Even though I am one and the same person who gets up in the morning and goes to sleep in the evening, I feel completely different at these two times. This is because I am actually different in the morning than in the evening. In the morning I am mostly hungry and feel the urge to move. In the evening, after a full day, I might need a sofa to rest and good music to relax. So I am not a fixed constant, but a constantly changing energy. And, I need food, exercise, sleep and much more during my entire lifetime in a cyclical, i.e. repetitive way.

In this respect, we could say that the "perceptual subject" resembles the state of consciousness that enables our wakefulness - and in a milder form also our dreaming - and distinguishes it from (deep) sleep.

This condensation of energy, which we have called 'the subject of perception', is only one end of a bipolar (two-pole) event, which we call perception. In a process of perception, the subject of perception is therefore nothing other than the perceiver or *receiver*.

b) Let's consider the moment in which we wake up, i.e. step out of deep sleep. For a certain short time we do not perceive anything specific because we are not focused on anything. But as awake consciousness we are already there!

It is very difficult to say what is meant by 'we' at this moment. Not to mention what is meant by 'we' during deep sleep! What is certain is:

Shortly after waking up our consciousness is there and we perceive nothing as long as our consciousness is focused on nothing. In the very moment it is focused, the "miracle" happens.

If we are awake enough, i.e. if the energy field we call consciousness reaches a sufficient level of excitement, then an arrangement of light stimuli, for example, can activate our sense of sight. More precisely:

A light stimulus (c) "touches" our sight. This stimulus is processed at lightning speed, and then received completely, because it appears or is projected on some "place" within our field of consciousness.

How do we experience this act? We have the feeling, firstly, that we are there, secondly, that something else is there, and thirdly, that we perceive this, i.e. that we are aware of it.

What is actually happening? By the activation of our sensual, i.e. all our sentient organs by the most different stimuli (c), a small or large part of our energetic consciousness field is formed to the event, which we call focusing.

The focusing of the consciousness thus arises from the fact that through our sensitive, sentient organs a dichotomy - a division into two - is established in the otherwise undifferentiated consciousness. We usually call this dichotomy the subject-object relationship. It is the basis of the possibility of our perception.

Raindrops, for example, are stimuli (c) that activate my sense of sight and touch. My visual and tactile faculty causes a division into two (into me and the rain) to be established in my field of consciousness, so that I can see and feel the rain. All my perceptive abilities are bundled on this event. They are gently and clearly directed towards it, focused on it.

Perception happens or rather *becomes possible* through a focusing of consciousness. This focusing of consciousness can now take different directions, depending on different causes. It can focus on a light stimulus or on a sound stimulus. It can be directed at an external complex event such as the behavior of certain people or at an internal emotional event. Therefore we can also speak of a <u>directionality of our perception</u> *beyond* a <u>focusing of consciousness</u>, which energetically enables an act of perception at all.

The *perception* of something is only made possible by the *focusing of consciousness*. And I perceive something *only* when my attention is *directed towards it*. 'Attention' means *directedness of consciousness* or *focused consciousness*.

PART II - What Is ADHD
*Really?*

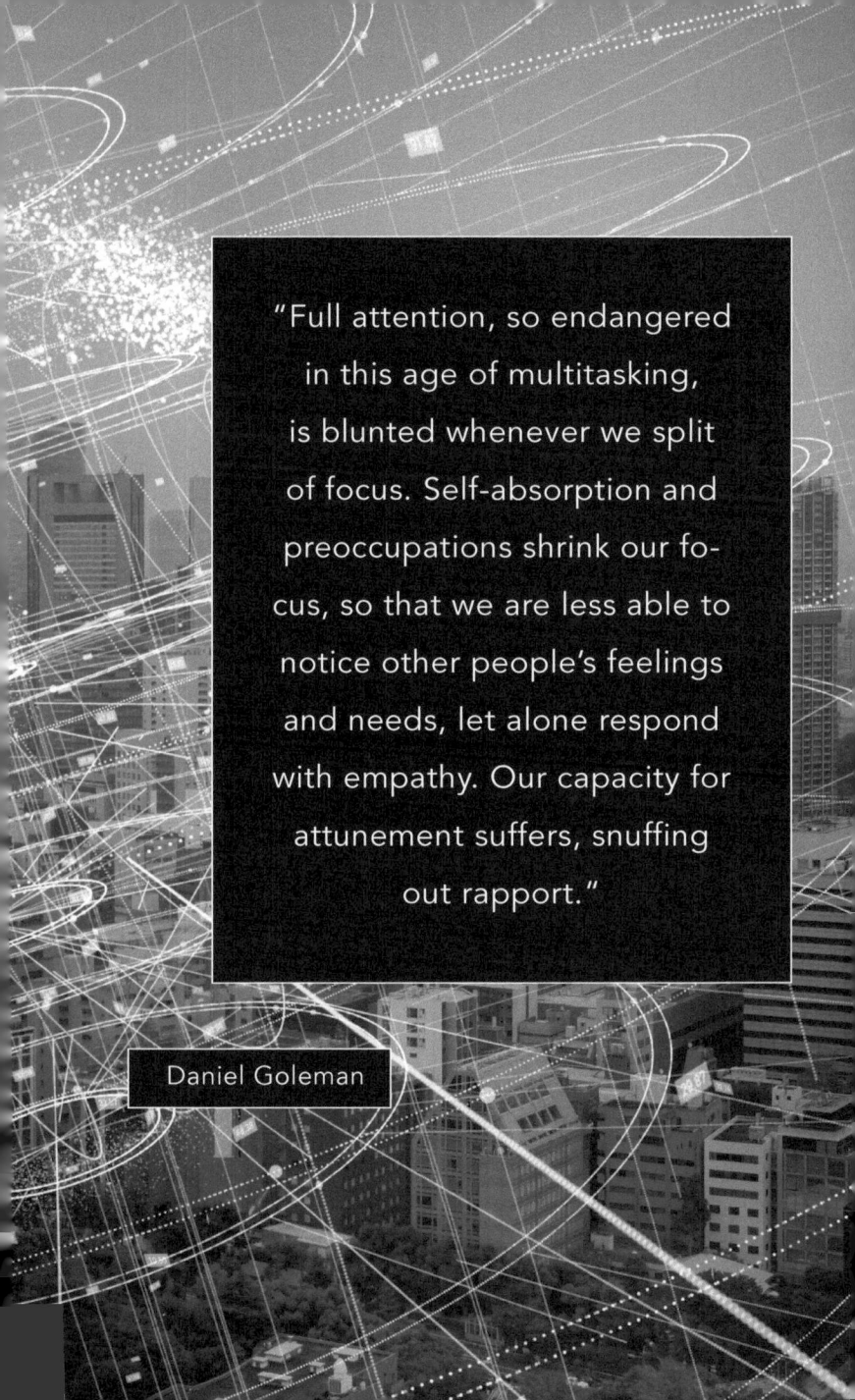

"Full attention, so endangered in this age of multitasking, is blunted whenever we split of focus. Self-absorption and preoccupations shrink our focus, so that we are less able to notice other people's feelings and needs, let alone respond with empathy. Our capacity for attunement suffers, snuffing out rapport."

Daniel Goleman

## 5. A Questionable "Creation"

In our metapostmodern times, a so-called disorder seems to be spreading massively. Well, at least it is diagnosed massively...

It is (as we will see in part III) a disturbance of inner tranquility or ease. It is so disturbed at its root that it has strong to alarming seismic effects on one of our most *important* abilities. What is meant is our *ability to pay attention*. Usually the said disturbance of inner calm is called Attention Deficit Hyperactivity Syndrome or Attention Deficit Hyperactivity Disorder or abbreviated: ADHD.

Already in the fifties scientists spoke of mental deficits in people who have difficulty being attentive, and especially in situations in which they are *expected* to be attentive. Later, they spoke of minimal brain dysfunction and hyperkinesis (excessive urge to move). In 1980, the American Psychiatric Society (APA) finally created the term Attention Deficit Disorder (ADD) for it. But in 1987, APA also saw this disorder as associated with hyperactivity, a condition that sometimes accompanies ADD. However, ADD and hyperactivity can also occur in isolation. When they occur together, they are called ADHD: Attention deficit hyperactivity disorder. Today, however, ADHD is (additionally) an inappropriate and uncontrollably impulsive behavior or an even more general inability to control one's own behavior...

Which symptoms are referred to as ADD or ADHD? These are forgetfulness, distractibility, nervousness and impatience, inner and outer restlessness, impulsiveness, difficulty in working, playing or speaking attentively or staying attentive long enough, difficulty in following instructions or completing tasks, and generally inappropriate social behavior.

If at least six of these or similar symptoms occur simultaneously and have a clearly problematic impact on areas such as work, school, coping with everyday life, human relationships or social behavior, APA speaks of ADD or ADHD.

# 6. What Is ADHD Really? Maybe An MDD?

We have (in Chapter 4) defined attention as "the directionality of focused consciousness". On the basis of this definition of attention, we now undertake the formulation of a definition of ADHD.

In habitual language use, an ADHD person is first of all referred to as "a person who is not attentive", without precise specification about what this exactly means.

The fact is that if we took this usage literally, ADHD would be a phantom problem according to our *definition* of attention. Because according to our preliminary considerations and our definition of attention, *everyone* is continuously attentive to something. In other words: One cannot be inattentive!

So if the expression "person X is not attentive" is not literally meant, how else can it be meant?

My first assumption as to how the expression "person X has ADHD" or "person X is not attentive" can be meant - formulated from my experience and work with ADHD "affected persons" - is that this person X is not attentive to a certain object Y, but to object Z, in a circumstance in which it is the task of this person X or is expected from this person X that this person X is attentive to this certain object Y and not to the object Z!

We could equate for example Y with a talking school teacher or with an office task and Z with an electronic game or with a holiday or leisure wish…

If this assumption is true, then we still cannot be sure that person X has ADHD. First of all, it may be that person X has not the slightest interest in being aware of object Y!

If so, then this is an *MDD* problem (MDD = Motivational Deficit Disorder). This is not an official expression or label, but one that I spontaneously formulated and in many cases the more apt or the only apt term.

Or it can be, secondly, that person X has a certain interest in object Y, but at the same time also has a clearly stronger interest in object Z. So here again there is no ADHD problem, but a slightly different variant or strength of an MDD problem.

How to treat MDD problems is certainly very important to know, but not the primary subject of this book.

Another possibility, how the expression "person X has ADHD" or "person X is not attentive" can be meant, has to do with the duration of the attention, in other words, with the attention span. Here it is the case that person X is aware of object Y (whether interested or not), but for various reasons cannot maintain this attention long enough or for as long as necessary and therefore inevitably turns to other objects (which promote *energetic, mental and emotional well-being*).

In such cases we also cannot talk about a real ADHD problem, because the reasons for the short attention span can either be due to lack of motivation or other reasons to be considered.

"But how is it possible that of the millions of people who have been diagnosed with ADHD, not a single one really has this disease? ...
In fact, not a single one is... But in all of this, it's amazing how we define this "disease" - based on its symptoms, not its causes...."

Richard Saul

# 7. Or Is ADHD actually An EDD?

The other area of supposed ADHD problems that I have come across with ADHD clients has to do with a disharmony in the energy balance. What exactly does that mean?

Let us first consider the very simple example that all of us know more or less when our attention keeps slipping away, when we are mentally challenged and at the same time simply tired or exhausted. It is very natural that we glide away, because we need a clear break or a longer recovery phase in such a moment.

In general: it is necessary to have sufficient and balanced energy and strength, distributed appropriately over the different activities of professional, school or general everyday life. Why balanced?

Firstly, the opposite can happen: not too little energy, but too much energy. This can result, for example, from the inappropriate use of different foods or from activities in which we are very moved internally - emotionally or, for example, through electronic games - and at the same time remain physically rather immobile!

Second, if there is also the possibility that we are not satisfactorily occupied enough, both through physical and mental activity, then we get into a possible energetic restlessness, implosion or "constipation".

All this inevitably leads to attention problems, but only due to *energetic imbalance* and *instability*. And then there is our "highly innovative" information and knowledge society with its myriads of stimuli, which stirs us up more and more or clog us additionally...

This all sounds very complex and multi-layered. Only, if it is a fact that all these causes confuse our attention understandably, then we all have to call these unnaturalities or natural contradictions by their specific *names* and not just *conjure up* an attention disturbance *speculatively*! Is that not so?

Without any doubt, we are dealing here with the causes of energetic dysfunction disorders (EDD; also a spontaneous term from me), which are indicators of an unhealthy life or a life that has come out of a somewhat natural river, which require corresponding changes and not artificial or behavioral military means to capture and suppress our living attention...

## 8. Or Is ADHD Maybe (Also) A CDD?

The last area of supposed (because not yet under-stood) ADHD problems, has to do with an *inability* to participate. It has to do with the inability to participate successfully or completely in a communication or knowledge acquisition process. More precisely, such a case occurs when someone, as a recipient of a commu-nicated content, experiences the problem of not being able to understand that content, let alone execute or practice it. The possible reasons for this:

1. The content is not understood by the person con-cerned because it is completely alien to him or her.

2. The content is not understood by the affected person because it is not completely familiar to him or her.

3. The content is not understood by the person con-cerned at all, or not understood with certainty, because the manner of its occurrence and/or presentation is either nebulous or strange, or cognitively dry and/or confused.

4. Consequently, such content cannot be mastered at all, not even practiced properly.

Such a content can be e.g. fractional arithmetic or an integral calculus. It can be a book that is important for an audit and at the same time is literally saturated with foreign words. It can be a complex management task that requires insight, overview, organization and flexibility!...

In all these cases it can therefore be due to a lack of understanding or not yet sufficiently acquired skills, so that despite the pious wish to concentrate on the respective task, one simply cannot (adequately or sufficiently) manage it.

If we would summarize the components 'understanding' and 'competence' under the general term 'ability' or 'competence', we would have to speak in these cases of a competence deficit disorder (CDD) and not of ADD or ADHD. AD(H)D would again not be an *Attention* Deficit (H) Disorder!...

"To be in the zone is to be in the deep heart of the Element. ...
We become focused and intent. We live in the moment. We become lost in the experience and perform at our peak. Our breathing changes, our minds merge with our bodies, and we feel ourselves drawn effortlessly into the heart of the Element."

Ken Robinson

PART III - ADHD *Decoded*

## 9. The Roots Of Attention Movement

"To control attention means to control the experience and thus the quality of life. Information only comes into consciousness when we are attentive to it. Attention serves as a filter of perception between the external events and their experience by us."

In this significant quotation from Csikszentmihalyi the importance of attention control is rightly explained. Apart from that, the formulation in the quotation may have the echo that attention is something separate from consciousness, something different or independent, and even able to decide what penetrates consciousness and what does not...

This is not the case because we have seen that attention is *secondary* to consciousness. Attention is merely the *term* for the *directedness of consciousness*.

Attention is consciousness! Not the other way around. Without consciousness attention dissolves into air! It *arises* only through a *focusing*, i.e. *directedness* of consciousness. And this consciousness is an energy field, which is only a part of the psychophysical energy volume, which constitutes us altogether. In this total volume, in which all living unconscious is also located, it is decided where our focused consciousness will be directed.

So when there is talk of things coming into consciousness by being aware of them, it means translated now: Things come into consciousness *when our consciousness is directed towards them*!

Csikszentmihalyi is absolutely right that there is a perception filter. However, it is interesting to examine what exactly is meant when we speak of directing attention. Not our attention is what filters, even if it may seem so at first glance, but it is ultimately and actually the causes that maneuver our attention, i.e. our focused consciousness, in one direction or the other. What attracts our consciousness in one direction or the other *is* what *does* the filtering.

For example, if I feel hunger, it is because my consciousness has been attracted to and directed toward the lack and therefore to the obtainment of food.

This is an energetic event within which biological-psychophysical mechanisms and processes determine, always synergistically with the respective total-organismic history of a living being, which need will "spur" perception into the possible directions of its fulfillment.

This energetic event determines our inner receptivity, of which M. Montessori speaks in the following:

"The inner receptivity determines what is to be absorbed from the diversity of the environment and which situations are the most advantageous for the current stage of development. It is it that causes the child to pay attention to certain things and not to others. As soon as such receptivity lights up in the child's soul, it is as if a ray of light emanates from it, illuminating only certain objects while leaving others in the dark. The whole perceptual world of the child is then suddenly limited to this one brightly lit area."

The more transparent the mentioned energetic event becomes to us, the better we can control our attention; the more transparent becomes to us how the movements of reality touch us. It is this touch that determines the energetic event by "disturbing" it and thereby creating energetic deficiencies, the so-called *needs*.

For example, by understanding that the feeling of hunger is due to a lack of food, I can ensure through a sufficient meal that this energetic deficiency is balanced and my need for food is satisfied. After eating, my consciousness is no longer attracted by the feeling of hunger, but is directed to something else, to another need that wants to be satisfied.

So the *needs* are the causes, the psychophysical

*roots* of the movements of our attention: hunger, thirst, fun, bliss, physical and mental well-being, mental challenge, meaningfulness of taking action, self-esteem, incessant satisfaction of curiosity; this is not a complete list, but a small attempt to indicate into which areas and dimensions we should listen and look if we are interested in finding the causes of the movements of our attention.

We can best control our attention when we learn to ensure the healthy and qualitative satisfaction of all our psychophysical needs, which are ultimately energetic disorders, through responsibility and organization!

But this satisfaction must not only and not only passively satisfy the presently existing or conscious needs, but possibly also all those who cannot even be awake because our being in its entirety may not yet have opened itself so far to be "disturbed" by the manifold - and insatiably abundant - movements of conditional reality!

## 10. The Life Fullness Deficit

There are two great failings in life that are possible...
The first is to be satisfied with less than life offers in all
its fullness. Because life is too big to play it small. And
if you play it small, then it "takes revenge"! Because it is
deeply and rightly "insulted".

If, for example, one does not come to feel oneself
completely, because social norms or the history of
one's parents have "prevented" one from it, then one
will only become acquainted with the depths, vastness,
and heights of human existence to a small degree...

If one has felt the life impulse in its indivisible
wholeness and wants to "allow" this impulse, this Élan
Vital the greatest possible expression, then the second
great possible failure consists in giving in to or chasing
after ways and means of expression, food and satisfaction which are alien to the wisdom inherent in life; ways
and means which do not agree with the nature of life
- its origin and the unchangeable natural-pure regular-
ities of its occurrence and existence.

For example, it is an unnatural behavior, alien to the
wisdom of life, to ignore a cold and to maintain one's
workload in spite of a listlessness, instead of giving the

body the much-needed rest and recovery.

About these two possible failings in life it must also be said that they can also take place unintentionally. This can happen, for example, when we grow up in a life culture and situation that does not fully meet both our natural needs and the sufficiently natural way in which those needs could be met.

For example, if a child is shown that grief and pain are "abnormal" and can be suppressed, it is very likely that the suppression of grief and pain will continue into adulthood, although this is unnatural. For grief and pain are as much a part of a person as joy and well-being and want to be expressed.

It is even worse if we are not (yet) aware of the fact that the two failings in life are taking place!

We could imagine an intensity scale of "suffering"; its intensity increases parallel to the accumulation of the above four circumstances: first failure (1), second failure (2), deficient life circumstances (3) and unconsciousness (4).

The suffering is most intense when all four circumstances are accumulated simultaneously.

If none of these circumstances is the case, that is, if the nature of life is corresponded to and completely harmonized with, and if this happens intentionally and consciously, then life shows itself in its fullness.

Let us now record what is hidden as the core of the problem in all four of the above circumstances: in all of these circumstances there is always either too much or too little of something.

The first failure brings with it a **lack of fullness of life** (1).

The second is a **lack** of natural or an abundance of unnatural **ways and means of expression, food and satisfaction** (2).

**Poor living conditions** (3) and a **lack of aware-ness** (4) can further increase the extent of the problem.

In this sense we could also speak of an imbalance or a lack of balance, a *lack of a holistic balance* of our *entire* life.

If this lack of equilibrium in our entire human psy-chophysical-organismic life *exceeds* the level of the bearable, then we are dealing with a disturbance, with a failure to find one's place and a failure to let one's natural state of life or life happen.

Such a disorder can indeed be considered and un-derstood as a serious problem, depending on the se-verity of the reduction in our well-being.

This type of disorder also includes the ADHD phe-nomenon or problem. If ADHD really is a problem,

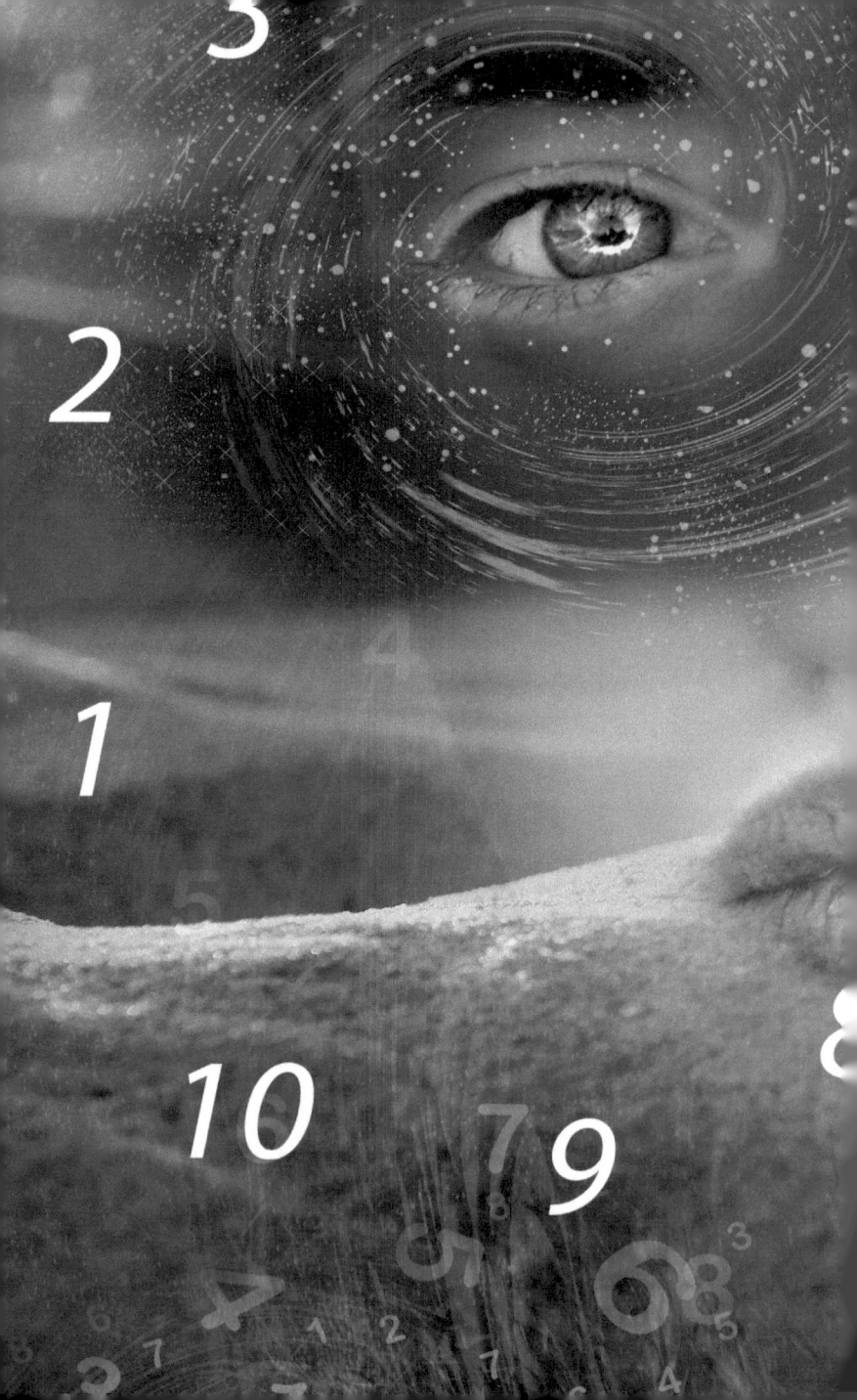

"All lives are different, and some face hardships that others will never know. But we all share the same universe, the same laws of nature, and the same fundamental task of creating meaning and of mattering for ourselves and those around us in the brief amount of time we have in the world.

Three billion heartbeats. The clock is ticking."

Sean Carroll

it can be solved by identifying and modifying the *sources* from which the *forces of movement* of our attention feed.

## 11. The Power Generators

Supposed ADHD manifestations can be hidden or even obvious motivation problems, i.e. a motivation deficit disorder (MDD) and/or force or energy problems, i.e. an energetic deficit disorder (EDD) and/or competence problems, i.e. a competence deficit disorder (CDD).

If we were to take this triple cause model apart and move into its deeper layers, we would get a complete overview of all generators of the forces and their regulating laws necessary for an intact and natural function of our attention.

I am aware that the possible scope of this deepening insight into the sources of stable, because all-encompassingly nourished attention actually goes beyond the scope of this chapter and is worthy of a longer essay. However, it will be briefly outlined to achieve a more complete understanding of ADHD, which includes both the *true* causes of ADHD *and* their transformation.

Both through my own ADHD "involvement" and through many years of working with ADHD clients of all ages and with a wide variety of ADHD initial causes, I have repeatedly identified the following - complementary and interacting - power generators that nourish a naturally healthy attention force or, if deficient or perhaps surplus, can lead to ADHD.

### Existential Reality

The first power generator in terms of its *scope* is rooted in the deepest level of our existence. It affects our state of mind and being most fundamentally, most primarily and most comprehensively.

For each of us it answers the questions: "Who or what am I?" and "What is reality and how does it work?" and "What is? What should I do? What do I have to do?".

Our existential - whether religious, spiritual or naturalistic - totality, situation and therefore also mood is the *brightest* and most translucent star of our psycho-physical universe, *shining through everything*.

If this (existential) source of power shows instabilities, then pretty much *everything* darkens, even if the other power generators were completely intact. But if it is in a state of *fullness*, then we are doing well, even if the other force generators could be relatively disturbed or weakened.

## Emotional Nourishment

Emotional and motivational nourishment is the second most important *power-generating component* of our stable well-being and our capacity for attention. This power generator is adequately fed when we live in *emotional freedom* and when we are *motivationally balanced*.

Emotional freedom means that (1) emotions have space and oxygen for their arising, their expression and their dissolution, and (2) we remove the breeding ground for a possible pathological and unnecessary emotionality through appropriate holistic growth. Motivational balance means that there is at least a balance between what we want or need and what we must, and that what we want is fulfilled and what we must is mastered. In addition, motivational balance can be properly anchored and take root when naturalness and freedom are the main "forces" to keep our life compass running. Emotional freedom and motivational balance are areas that (can) exert tremendous power on our attention.

## Energetic Balance

This is about the knowledge and awareness of the

importance of sufficient and qualitative energy. This means both the power of movement we need to tackle our activities from the full, as well as the sufficient consumption of excess energy.

The two keys to energetic wisdom are food and movement; both in a general sense: physical, mental and emotional. So it is about the wisdom of multidimensional energy experience, both in its receiving and in its powering out/consuming character; both in the nourishment-wanting of our lack of energy as well as in the consumption-and-unfolding-wanting of our excess energy.

## Mental Clarity

Already in our childhood, we all unfortunately developed, through the invitation of adults, the habit of concentrating excessively whenever we do not understand something or are overwhelmed by a content or a task. This *strains* our attention!

The problem with this is that we are very rarely aware of this habit, because it always disguises itself very subtly and quickly as a strength of perception. However, this problem is also representative for all mental struggles and ambiguities and overloads that consume our strength.

The solution, on the other hand, is to become conscious and assume responsibility in all those areas in which we have gaps in understanding and competence and which are of vital importance for us personally and professionally.

So that we fully understand what is not yet clear and fully internalize what we have not yet learned.

So that we develop a realistic feeling and management for what is still to be learned, what is still to be known and what is still to be lived.

So that our mind is permeated with clarity in all its challenges and in all its preferences and in all its both free and purposeful activity.


### Organismic Action

The last power generator mentioned here naturally results from the others.

If all other four power generators *are* in order, then our life will look in order if the fact of a basic existential-emotional-energetic-mental nourishment reveals to us a corresponding intelligent *action*. The more completely and clearly we can stand in reality through the other force generators, the more stably and smoothly we can walk.

This may sound abstract and very general, but the

four other power generators *do* provide food and knowledge *on all levels*. We can, based on this, now *act* as this is *necessary* (1), or we (can) *know* when it is *not* necessary to act (2). And this both organismically:

*Organismic* action is doing, creating or being active, which both *naturally* appears out of us and *automatically* sets itself in motion and takes place in compliance with and by fulfilling all the laws of *reality* that *enable*, *determine* and *realize* human organismic existence.

Everyone may want to *know* what (only) is and what is to *be done*. If knowledge is *lacking*, then such knowledge must *at first* be found. But *then*, what is necessary, is *action*.

*No one*, who *has* the necessary knowledge, may "complain", who does *not* get or experience or is what can *only* manifest itself *through his action*.

## 12. The Common Key

If we seriously consider all sources of power of our attention - existential reality, emotional nourishment, energetic balance, mental clarity and organismic action - we will conclude, among other things, that all these sources of power affect *each* of us, and that *none* or very *few* of us all have these power generators working *flawlessly*. Does that then mean that we are *ADHD sufferers*?...

The causes of well-being and behavioral phenomena referred to as ADHD result from a lack of quality or activity, or excess activity of the aforementioned power generators. The consequence of this is that the respective needs in the respective areas of life are not met sufficiently or *not at all* or *incorrectly*.

Unfulfilled needs lead to inner *restlessness*. This can be more stormy or gentler, depending on the strength of the unfulfilled needs. The more stormy, i.e. stronger, the more likely it is that such behavior will be labeled *ADHD*.

This restlessness *is the common key* to all the causes that move our attention.

This restlessness is positive when it is important for

our well-being that our attention is focused on certain things in order to meet natural and healthy needs.

It is negative when it arises from unfulfillable or false or illusory needs.

It is just as negative when appropriate needs are met with the wrong measures - and sometimes in excess!

In all these three cases there is no attention deficit or no true ADHD, but a fulfillment deficit of certain needs! This is not a play on words, but a serious fact; and unfortunately it does not yet answer the question why one speaks of *attention deficit* or *hyperactivity* or *impulsiveness* or *problematic behavior* syndrome... Why must a behavioral *action*, i.e. a *symptom*, be seen as the syndrome or disorder and not the true disorder, i.e. the source or cause of the problem?

If one were to ask oneself what would be the more appropriate name for the symptoms that many people are currently throwing under ADHD, then the questions should rather be: "What do you call an *emotional food* deficit?" or "What do you call a *learning success* deficit?" or "What do you call an *everyday structure* deficit?" and so on. The directly safe, common and primary answer to all these questions? *Not* ADHD!

Should we, however, since it is not primarily about the name, but about the thing, want to resign ourselves to using the term ADHD for behaviors that lead to a more or less *problematic* lack of control over the functioning and movement of our attention due to *inner restlessness*, then it is already important to know what this inner restlessness actually wants to *tell* us in the core and overall...

"What exhausts us is the non-use of the possibilities of our organs and our senses, their deactivation, their suppression... What invigorates is unfolding. Unfolding through the confrontation with a world that challenges me as a whole."

Hugo Kükelhaus

PART IV - The Ingredients
Of *Fulfillment*

## 13. The Message Of ADHD

ADHD is a blessing because it communicates to us – in an outspoken and direct manner – a need that needs to be heard and understood. It is a healthy and urgent *reaction* to the *self-alienation* that human world development wants to impose on us (controlled or unintentionally).

ADHD behavior is a reaction of mentally and emotionally healthy people who decisively resist to what is going wrong. An ADHD behavior is an inner cry: "Dear world, I don't feel well in you and that worries me deeply. I don't know what to do... Help!"

Plato sums it up with simple words. He speaks of life that is contrary to nature:

"Where the diseases originate from is probably obvious to everyone. For since there are four areas from which the body is joined together, earth, fire, water, and air, it is the lack or abundance of them that is contrary to nature, as well as the exchange of the place to which one is entitled with a place alien to him."

Thus, according to Plato, a life contrary to nature leads to an abundance and/or a lack and/or sometimes even a misuse and therefore to a confusion of life forces.

ADHD is such a fundamental *confusion* or an *erroneous mixing ratio of natural life energy*.

ADHD is the result of a lifestyle that is bombarded and polluted by a variety of unnaturalities.

Adult ADHD sufferers may be able to become aware of ADHD on their own, perhaps with some help from others.

However, children and adolescents affected by ADHD almost always need the help, knowledge and support of adults.

In both cases, ADHD can be completely resolved in its "negativity" and completely controlled in its "positivity".

This is done in a natural way by purifying and reordering the sources of our attention force - existential reality, emotional nourishment, energetic balance, mental clarity and organismic action - so that their self-sustaining cycle naturally flows and nourishes itself through a feeling life.

If the laws of nature are disregarded in purifying and reordering these sources, ADHD will not dissolve.

The ADHD event is a strong indication of the need to meditate and contemplate on the true content of the terms 'nature', 'natural' and 'disturbance', to penetrate it through true science and deep understanding, and to do justice to it through a *truly natural life*.

This would not only give us the solution for ADHD, but significantly more. We would already be standing with one foot in the realm of fullness.

# 14. The Dimensions Of Nourishment

By *food* we usually mean physical food. When we ingest it, it transforms into forms of energy that in a variety of ways guarantee our entire physical manifest existence. A sufficient quantity as well as quality is required. Then we are well nourished and we also feel this way.

In the figurative sense, however, there is also emotional and also mental and also existential nourishment. We need all these forms of nourishment in order to experience a holistic well-being.

If the types of food necessary for us are *inadequately* or *incorrectly fulfilled*, the resulting *inner restlessness* (among other things) causes a disturbance in the way we move our *attention*.

In my understanding a *disturbance* is the non-taking-place and non-letting-be of the *natural* state or happening of something.

*Natural* is something, which corresponds to the nature of itself and coincides *totally* with it, is in *complete harmony* with it.

And nature is the origin of something, including the unchangeable laws of its happening and existence. It shows what something really is and how it really is.

### The Nourishing Dimension of Reality

Existential reality is a dimension of nourishment that can be either unconscious or elusive. It is so primary and omnipresent and all-encompassing that we cannot easily grasp it. For it is not an object. It is all space and all context in which both *we* and *everything else* as well as the *entire* known and imagined world are *contained*.

It always appears when we have a reasonably unambiguous perception or knowledge of what reality means, both *reality* and *our* reality. And what we perceive and recognize determines the basic quality and therefore also the most primary food of our existence, our being, our being there.

The meaning of this dimension of nourishment therefore arises directly as soon as it is recognized and permeates (through what it is) everything.

### The Emotional Dimension of Nourishment

Psychical or emotional nourishment comes from

"...For insofar as we are intelligent beings, we can only desire that which is necessary, and we can only be fully satisfied with that which is true. If we therefore recognize this correctly, then the aspiration of the better part of us coincides with the order of all nature."

Benediktus de Spinoza

our emotional life. Our emotional life is what the totality of our experience does with us emotionally.

Our emotional life concerns our emotional relationship to everything. To what we do. To what we do but do not want. To what we want but do not do or do not allow. To others. To what happens. To what is. To reality and all its facets. And to ourselves, *too*, or even *more* so.

Emotionally we are nourished when our feeling becomes or is free, so that the event that psychically defines and determines us can be realized according to its nature.

**Energetic Nourishment**

The next important dimension of food or nourishment is the nature of the energy that constitutes and determines us.

If it is agreed that everything (manifested) is energy, so *are we*. Regardless of the fact that the forms of energy we are as a whole are more gross or subtle, and physical, emotional or mental.

We are energy, we absorb energy, we are transforming energy, and we consume energy.

We absorb and consume physical, emotional and mental energy.

For this we must or can or should actively, awakely and sensitively take responsibility, preferably within the framework of our possibilities and in accordance with the corresponding laws of reality.

## The Nourishing Dimension Of The Mind

In order to achieve the mental nourishment that is *jointly* responsible for the healthy movement of our attention, we need clear knowledge.

This is about information and internalization:

Which knowledge do I need for what?

What types of knowledge are there?

Which areas of knowledge are there?

How much of all the necessary knowledge do I already have?

How do I still get the knowledge that I lack?

Which knowledge do I only have to internalize mentally and which must I incorporate through practice so that it becomes certain ability?

These and other such questions must receive a

clear *answer*. Only *then* are we mentally clear, relaxed and free. Only then can we clearly perceive our responsibility, accept it and *act* purposefully.

## 15. The Well-Organized Life

All dimensions of nourishment that we need or that constitute us are not separate from each other, but always organismic parts of a *wholeness*. We *are* this wholeness. We are a emotional-energetic-mental wholeness that exists *in this universe*, that is, in a reality with a certain *constitution* and certain *laws* of being and becoming.

We are a emotional-energetic-mental happening and experiencing, which does not float alone in nothingness, but exists in an all-encompassing *reality* and even *emerges* from it.

ADHD dissolves and disappears in a life in which all dimensions of our wholeness are *organismically seamlessly connected* with each other, i.e. are *organized*, i.e. are *arranged with each other* in such a way that they *fulfill* what and how and for what we are *meant* to be as an organism.

From this it follows that our task is an organizational one. We must provide the food of all dimensions that nourish and sustain us, and this in a way in which the different types of food are organically and organismically combined, so that together they fulfill their overall purpose, namely our well-being, our being nourished, our being fulfilled. *That* is our task. *That* is what we must fulfill. And this through our *actions*.

If well-being, nourishment and fulfillment are not undoubtedly guaranteed in the Basic Law or in the constitution of human coexistence, this would still have to happen. And that for *all* living things. Not only for fellow human beings.

*Why* for all living things? Because all *living* manifestation is of *living* things.

What (therefore) could only be missing for organizing our fulfillment would be the sufficient intelligence *of togetherness*.

Everyone, everyone and every living thing has the right *to be free*, especially in determining their own fulfillment.

This freedom has *limits*. Its limits begin and end exactly at the point where someone *else's* freedom is violated or disturbed.

*Such* knowledge, about how the <u>freedom</u> of an *individual* living being with the <u>being-together</u>-of-living beings-with-each-other <u>can be harmonized</u>, is the intelligence of togetherness.

## 16. Attention and Fulfillment

"Through the coming together of our impulse to satisfaction with the state of the absolute equilibrium, which can never be reached psychophysically due to the laws of reality, the feeling that something is missing and keeps us away from the absolute equilibrium constantly arises in us. We call the feeling of this state of deficiency 'need'".

Need is therefore the *feeling* that something is missing and that we therefore need it and that we therefore automatically want it. For example water. Thirst is the feeling of *lack*, which means the need for *water*.

It is self-explanatory that an <u>inner restlessness</u> always arises seamlessly in the moment in which I do <u>not get</u> something I <u>need</u>, e.g. water, without which I feel thirst. And the *longer* the lack of what I *need* lasts, the stronger my inner *restlessness* becomes. Is it not true?

And isn't it just as obvious that my consciousness will focus *on* what and where *water* is?

Attention is the *directedness of consciousness*. It embodies the turning of our *feeling towards* what is *needed*.

If *nothing is needed* for a moment or longer, and

nothing needs to be noticed, then the attention *rests*.

That which is *unconscious* and takes place, we do not "have to" notice.

Experiencing or living means feeling. Feeling takes place within consciousness. What is felt is what consciousness focuses on, i.e. we become aware of it, i.e. we perceive it.

We can only want that which we feel we need.

If we feel that we need something, we can feel it in a non-tensed, free state.

Fulfillment exists when the will that constitutes us is satisfied, i.e. well nourished.

The will that constitutes us is the totality of all our needs. The way to fulfillment is *knowing* all our needs, that is, the *will* that constitutes us, and all organized *action* that *satisfies* that will.

Our most *faithful companion* on the way to fulfillment is our attention.

**Ennealogue  Of The Attentive Life**

An Outline

"We mark with light in the memory the few interviews we have had, in the dreary years of routine and of sin, with souls that made our souls wiser; that spoke what we thought; that told us what we knew; that gave us leave to be what we inly were."

Ralph Waldo Emerson

# Ennealogue Of The Attentive Life

An Outline

"During Carl Rogers' stays in Hamburg at the beginning of the eighties of the last century, it was impressive to see how lightly, lovingly and sincerely the now eighty-year-old arranged his therapeutic and human encounters. It probably takes a lifelong learning to express elementary human sides, to become as simple, compassionate and real as he is, to be able to entrust oneself to the stream of events of one's own ideas, thoughts and feelings in contact with other people."

It would take at least one more book to pay appropriate tribute to Inghard Langer's (1943-2013) homage to Carl R. Rogers.

On the other hand, it is less difficult for me to pay tribute to Inghard Langer myself with the same (above) words. I had the honor and the immeasurable luck to spend some time with Inghard, even if a rather short one, and this gave me, compared to other corresponding experiences, so much that it would not even be measurable in decades... Why?

He embodied a biotic energy field that I had never known before; a space of life energy in which openness, presence, feeling, perception and communication manifested themselves fluently and seamlessly in a "nutritiously" very satisfying degree of vibration.

And, of course, I would like to mention that Inghard's attention was both *completely on* and *there* and clearly and completely *focused on the matter*, on several levels *simultaneously*....

From the background of such an example, I introduce the following Ennealogue Of The Attentive Life.

## Ennealogue Of The Attentive Life

*I am, so I feel.*

*I feel, so I am - conscious(ly).*

*I am energy and space.*

*I breathe freely and naturally.*

*What disturbs this breathing, I perceive.*

*I eliminate such disturbances by acting.*

*What nourishes my breathing, I perceive.*

*I get such food by acting.*

*I feel free...*

## Citations

In the order they appear in this book.

---------------------------------------------------------------------------------

07 *I don't know:* Gleick (2014), 8

11 *He carved:* Gleick (2014), 18

11 *While his:* Neffe (2006), 29

14 *To control attention:* Csikszentmihalyi (1999), 168

27 *Every one knows:* James (1890), 403-404

35 *Full attention:* Goleman (2007), 88

42 *But how is it possible:* Saul (2015), 19-20

48 *To be in the zone:* Robinson (2009), 87

51 *To control attention:* Csikszentmihalyi (1999), 168

53 *The inner receptivity:* Montessori (1987), 51-52

59 *All lives:* Carroll (2017), 433

70 *What exhausts us:* Kükelhaus (1978), 14

73 *Where the diseases:* Platon, *Timaios,* 82a

78 *For insofar as:* Spinoza, *Ethik,* IV, Anhang, Hauptsatz 32.

85 *Through the coming:* Tzivanakis (2006), 23

89 *We mark with light:* Emerson (1838)

91 *During Carl Rogers' stays:* Langer & Langer (2005), 88

# Literature

**Carroll**, Sean, *The Big Picture*, New York 2017.

**Csikszentmihalyi**, Mihaly, *Lebe gut! (Finding Flow)* Stuttgart 1999.

**Emerson**, Ralph Waldo, *Divinity School Address*, 1838.

**Gleick**, James, *Isaac Newton*, Düsseldorf 2014.

**Goleman**, Daniel, *Social Intelligence*, London 2007.

**James**, William, *The Principles of Psychology*, New York 1890: Henry Holt, Vol. 1.

**Kükelhaus**, Hugo, *Fassen, Fühlen, Bilden*. Organerfahrungen im Umgang mit Phänomenen, Köln 1978.

**Langer & Langer**, *Jugendliche begleiten und beraten*, München 2005.

**Montessori**, Maria, *Kinder sind anders*, München 1987.

**Neffe**, Jürgen, *Einstein*, Reinbek bei Hamburg 2006.

**Platon**, *Timaios*, 82a.

**Robinson**, Ken, *The Element*, London 2009.

**Saul**, Richard, *Die ADHS-Lüge (ADHD does not exist)*, Stuttgart 2015.

**Spinoza,** Benediktus de, *Ethik*, Teil IV, Anhang, Hauptsatz 32.

**Tzivanakis**, Ioannis, *Über das Wollen*, im Lernintelligenz-Magazin Nr. 0, Hamburg 2006.

# About The Author

---

Ioannis Tzivanakis was born in Greece in 1966. He spent his early childhood in Germany, then completed primary school and high school in Greece, returned to Germany in 1985 and studied **linguistics** and **philosophy of language**  at the University of Bremen. His focus was on **semantics**, **consciousness research** and **wholeness**.

Since 1996 he has worked as a trainer and learning consultant in the areas of **learning intelligence**, **learning problems**, **dyslexia**, **dyscalculia** and **ADHD** in Germany, France and other European countries.

In 2006 and 2007 he published four issues of the **Learning Intelligence Magazine** on foundations of **learning**, **learning intelligence**, **management** and **spirituality**.

His book "**Schulasthenie**" (dysschoolia) was published in 2013.

Further information can be found on the Internet:
**www.tzivanakis.com**